EXTREME ENGINEERING

PETRA

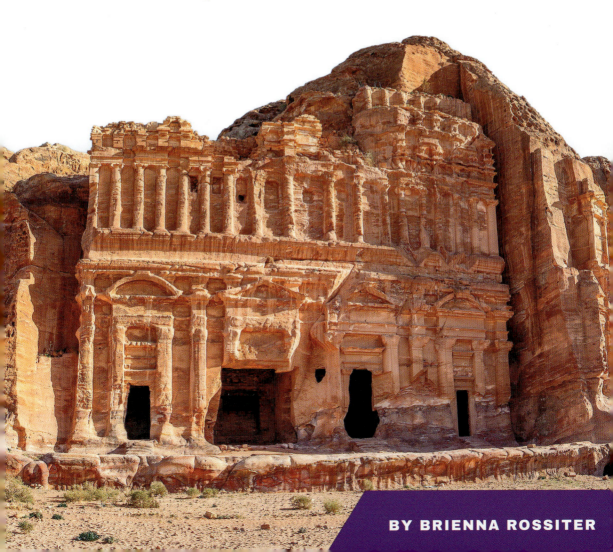

BY BRIENNA ROSSITER

WWW.APEXEDITIONS.COM

Copyright © 2024 by Apex Editions, Mendota Heights, MN 55120. All rights reserved. No part of this book may be reproduced or utilized in any form or by any means without written permission from the publisher.

Apex is distributed by North Star Editions:
sales@northstareditions.com | 888-417-0195

Produced for Apex by Red Line Editorial.

Photographs ©: Shutterstock Images, cover, 1, 4–5, 6, 7, 8, 9, 10–11, 12, 13, 14, 14–15, 16–17, 18–19, 20, 21, 22–23, 24–25, 26–27, 29

Library of Congress Control Number: 2023910874

ISBN
978-1-63738-752-8 (hardcover)
978-1-63738-795-5 (paperback)
978-1-63738-879-2 (ebook pdf)
978-1-63738-838-9 (hosted ebook)

Printed in the United States of America
Mankato, MN
012024

NOTE TO PARENTS AND EDUCATORS

Apex books are designed to build literacy skills in striving readers. Exciting, high-interest content attracts and holds readers' attention. The text is carefully leveled to allow students to achieve success quickly. Additional features, such as bolded glossary words for difficult terms, help build comprehension.

CHAPTER 1
STONE CITY 4

CHAPTER 2
PETRA'S HISTORY 10

CHAPTER 3
BUILDING PETRA 16

CHAPTER 4
LEARNING ABOUT PETRA 22

COMPREHENSION QUESTIONS • 28
GLOSSARY • 30
TO LEARN MORE • 31
ABOUT THE AUTHOR • 31
INDEX • 32

CHAPTER 1

STONE CITY

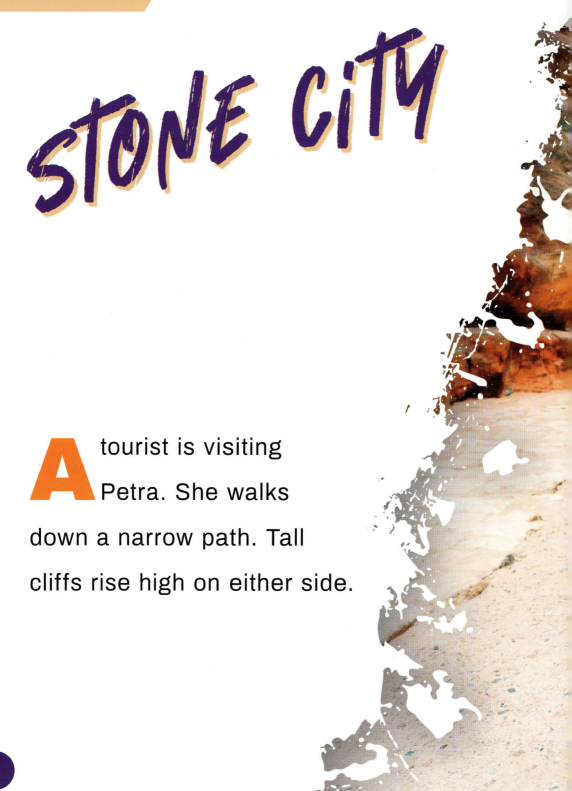

A tourist is visiting Petra. She walks down a narrow path. Tall cliffs rise high on either side.

The road leading into Petra is called the Siq.

Suddenly, the path widens. The tourist sees a huge building. It's carved into the **canyon** wall. A large city lies beyond it. The streets and buildings are made of stone.

The first building that visitors to Petra see is called the Treasury.

Many people think the Treasury was once a temple or grave.

RED ROCKS

Petra means "rock" in Greek. Much of the city is made from sandstone. This soft rock is often a reddish color. So, Petra is sometimes called "the rose-colored city."

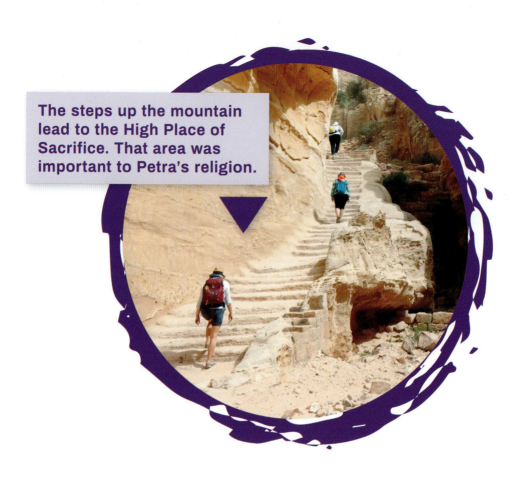

The steps up the mountain lead to the High Place of Sacrifice. That area was important to Petra's religion.

The tourist spends all day exploring. She visits dozens of **tombs** and temples. She also follows steps up a mountain. She enjoys many stunning views.

FAST FACT
Petra has a huge outdoor theater. It is carved into a mountain.

Petra has more than 500 tombs, temples, and homes. Visiting all of them would take days.

CHAPTER 2

PETRA'S HISTORY

Petra is a city in Jordan. No one knows when it was first built. But by 312 BCE, it was the capital of the Nabataean Empire.

The Nabataean Empire began rising to power around 200 BCE.

The Nabataeans used Petra for trade. By 100 BCE, the city was large and powerful.

Two important trade routes passed through Petra. Traders moved goods to and from Egypt, Arabia, China, and India.

Between 10,000 and 30,000 people may have once lived in Petra.

WORKING WITH WATER

Petra is in the desert. Rain rarely falls. When it does rain, floods are common. The Nabataeans used **engineering** to solve both problems. They built dams and channels to catch and store water.

Earthquakes in 363 CE and 551 CE damaged large parts of the city. But some stone buildings survived.

Petra became part of the Roman Empire in 106 CE. Later, the city faced **earthquakes** and changing trade routes. People began leaving. By the 700s, Petra was abandoned.

FAST FACT

For a time, Petra was part of the Byzantine Empire.

The Monastery may have been built as a tomb. Later, the Byzantines likely used it as a church.

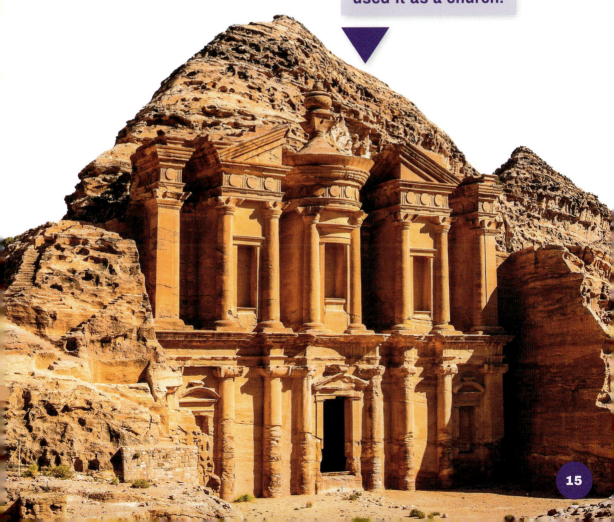

CHAPTER 3

BUILDING PETRA

Many parts of Petra are carved into rock walls. Builders dug caves to create rooms. They carved **facades** at the fronts.

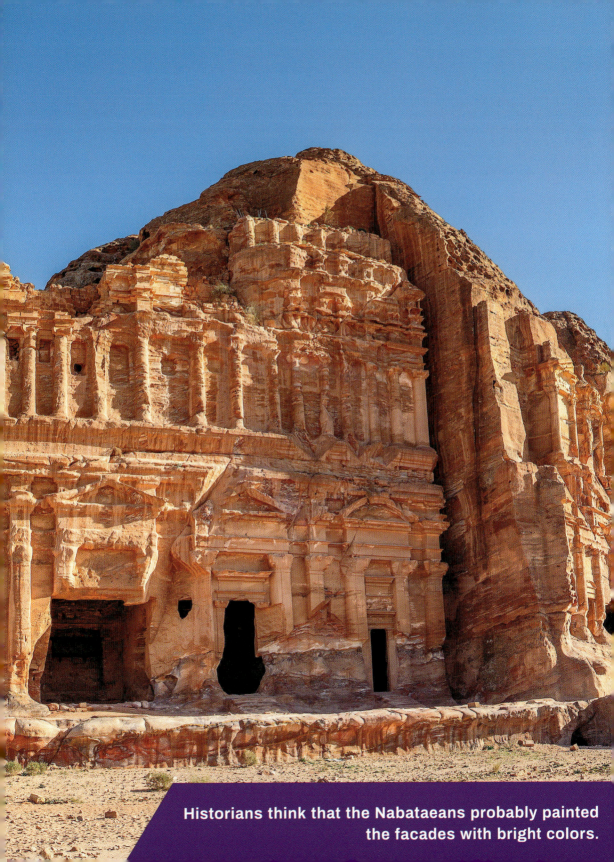

Historians think that the Nabataeans probably painted the facades with bright colors.

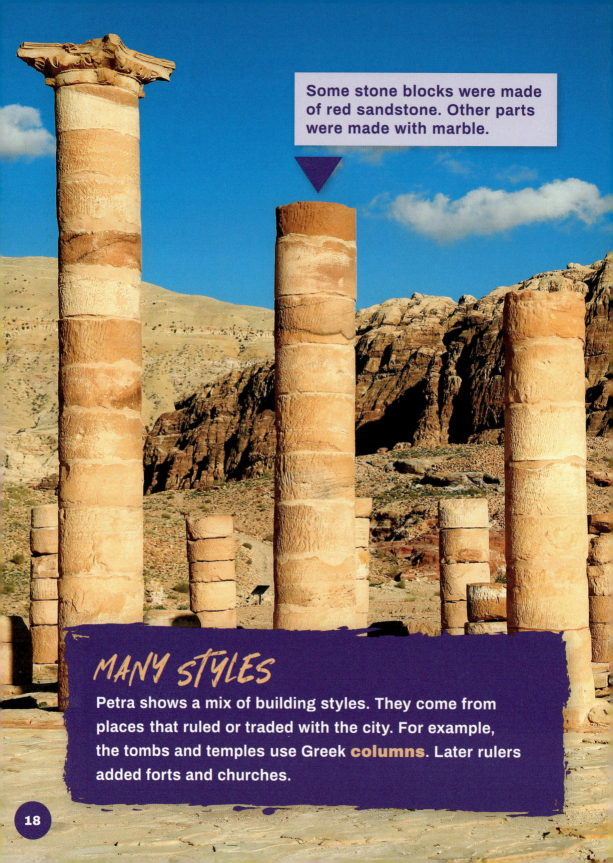

Some stone blocks were made of red sandstone. Other parts were made with marble.

MANY STYLES

Petra shows a mix of building styles. They come from places that ruled or traded with the city. For example, the tombs and temples use Greek **columns**. Later rulers added forts and churches.

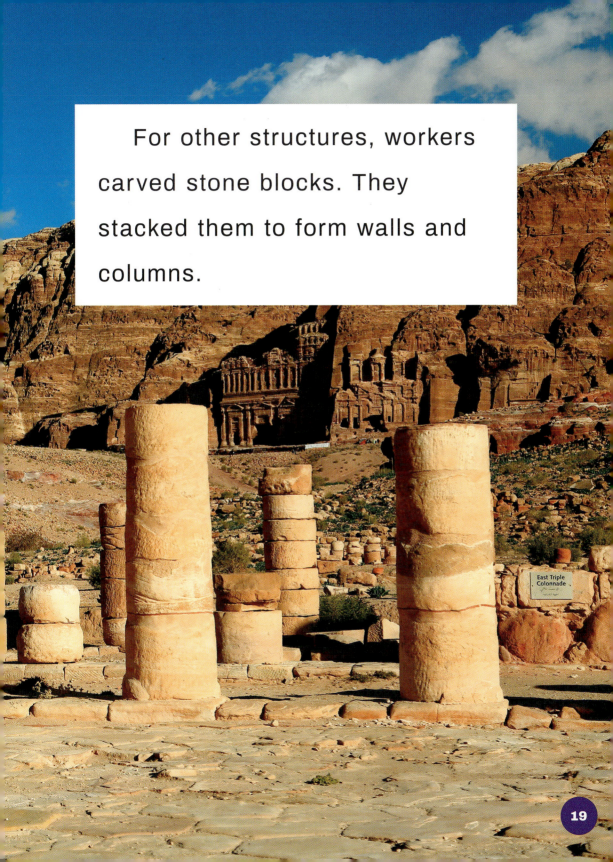

For other structures, workers carved stone blocks. They stacked them to form walls and columns.

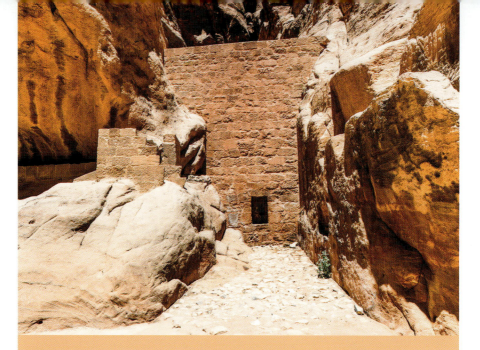

Dams and channels helped protect the city from flooding.

Workers built dams. They also cut channels to guide water through the city. Some channels held clay pipes. **Cisterns** stored water for later use.

Some channels were built alongside paths.

FAST FACT

The road into Petra had channels along its walls. The channels brought water from a spring 5 miles (8 km) away.

CHAPTER 4

LEARNING ABOUT PETRA

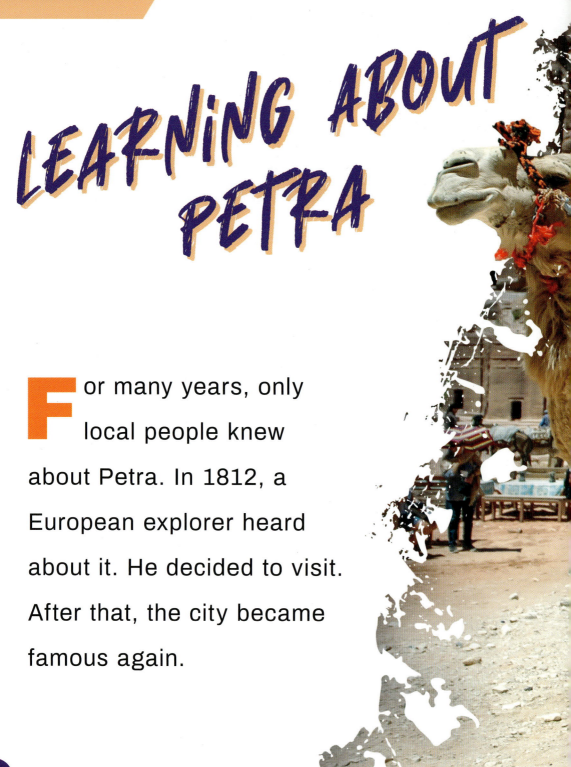

For many years, only local people knew about Petra. In 1812, a European explorer heard about it. He decided to visit. After that, the city became famous again.

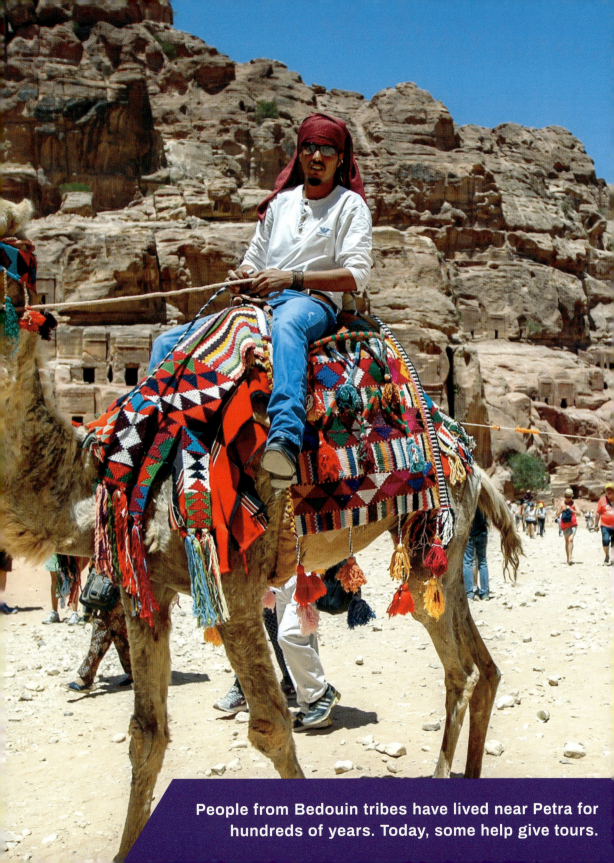

People from Bedouin tribes have lived near Petra for hundreds of years. Today, some help give tours.

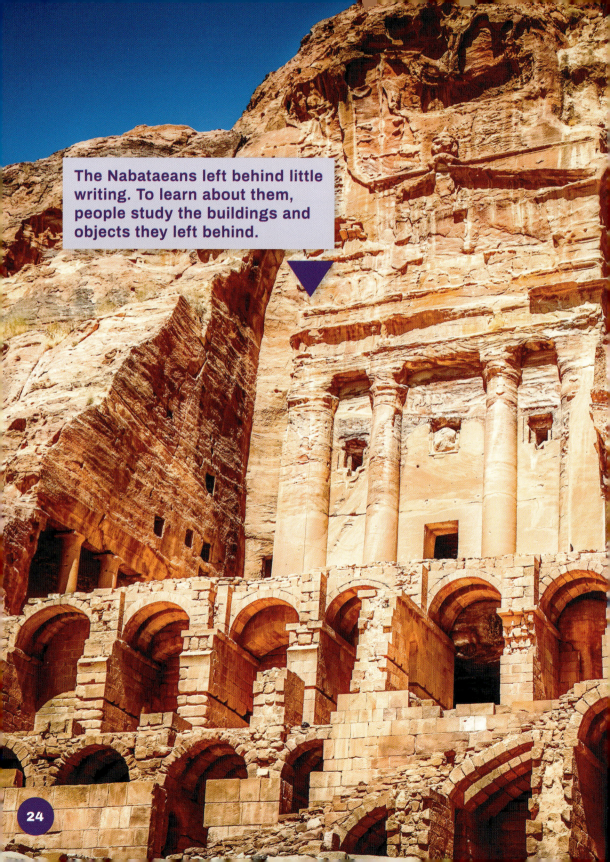

The Nabataeans left behind little writing. To learn about them, people study the buildings and objects they left behind.

Starting in the 1900s, people did **excavations**. They learned about the city and its past.

FAST FACT

One dig helped people learn the city's original name. It was called Raqeem.

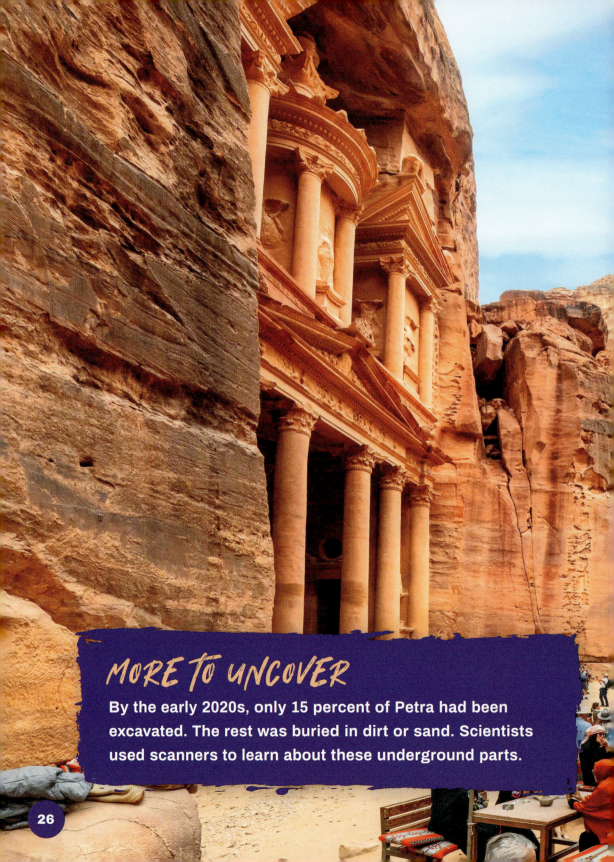

MORE TO UNCOVER

By the early 2020s, only 15 percent of Petra had been excavated. The rest was buried in dirt or sand. Scientists used scanners to learn about these underground parts.

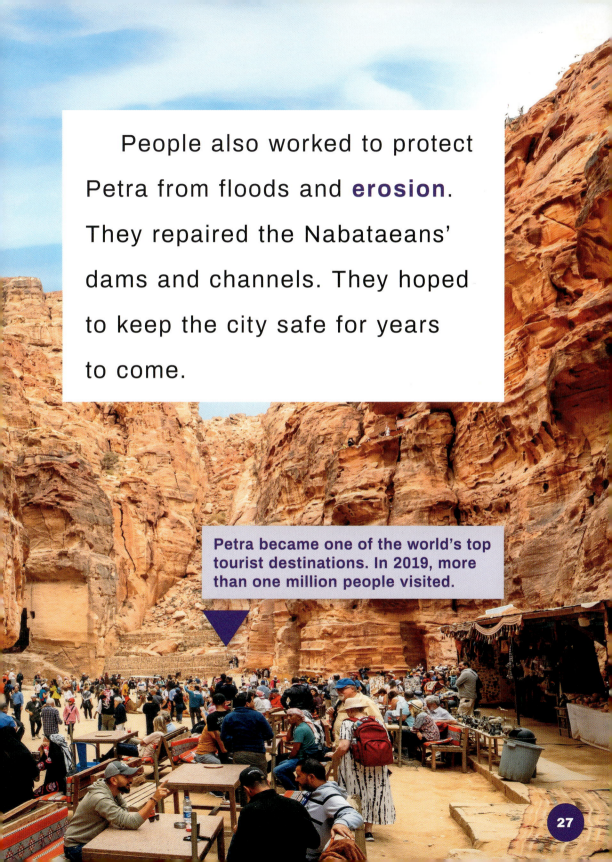

People also worked to protect Petra from floods and **erosion**. They repaired the Nabataeans' dams and channels. They hoped to keep the city safe for years to come.

Petra became one of the world's top tourist destinations. In 2019, more than one million people visited.

COMPREHENSION QUESTIONS

Write your answers on a separate piece of paper.

1. Write a few sentences that explain the main ideas of Chapter 2.

2. If you went to Petra, what part would you most want to see? Why?

3. Which empire was Petra the capital of?
    - **A.** Byzantine Empire
    - **B.** Roman Empire
    - **C.** Nabataean Empire

4. How would repairing Petra's dams and channels help prevent floods?
    - **A.** The dams and channels control where water flows.
    - **B.** The dams and channels stop all water.
    - **C.** The dams and channels would be gone.

5. What does **abandoned** mean in this book?

*People began leaving. By the 700s, Petra was **abandoned**.*

    A. empty of people
    B. full of people
    C. full of water

6. What does **spring** mean in this book?

*The road into Petra had channels along its walls. The channels brought water from a **spring** 5 miles (8 km) away.*

    A. a time of year
    B. a coiled piece of metal
    C. a source of water

Answer key on page 32.

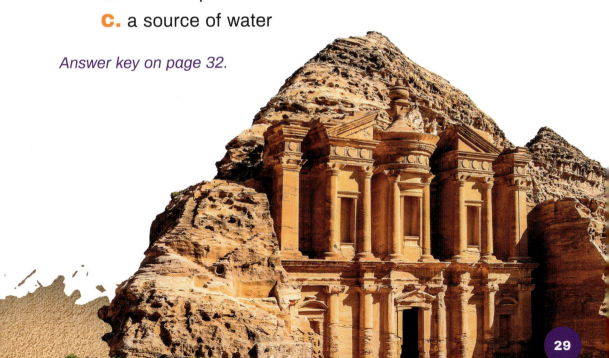

29

GLOSSARY

canyon
A deep cut in the ground that has steep sides.

cisterns
Pools or tanks that store water.

columns
Parts of buildings that are shaped like tall tubes. They often hold things up.

earthquakes
Events where parts of Earth shake or tremble.

engineering
Using math and science to solve problems.

erosion
When something slowly wears away over time.

excavations
Projects to dig something out of the ground.

facades
Front parts of buildings, especially fancy ones.

tombs
Places that mark where dead people are buried.

BOOKS

Murray, Julie. *Petra*. Minneapolis: Abdo Publishing, 2022.

Oachs, Emily Rose. *Pompeii*. Minneapolis: Bellwether Media, 2020.

Spanier, Kristine. *Petra*. Minneapolis: Jump!, 2021.

ONLINE RESOURCES

Visit **www.apexeditions.com** to find links and resources related to this title.

ABOUT THE AUTHOR

Brienna Rossiter is a writer and editor who lives in Minnesota.

INDEX

B
Byzantine Empire, 15

C
carved, 6, 9, 16, 19
channels, 13, 20–21, 27

D
dams, 13, 20, 27

E
excavations, 25

J
Jordan, 10

M
mountain, 8–9

N
Nabataean Empire, 10, 12–13, 27

R
Raqeem, 25
Roman Empire, 14

S
sandstone, 7
scanners, 26

T
temples, 8, 18
tombs, 8, 18

ANSWER KEY:
1. Answers will vary; 2. Answers will vary; 3. C; 4. A; 5. A; 6. C